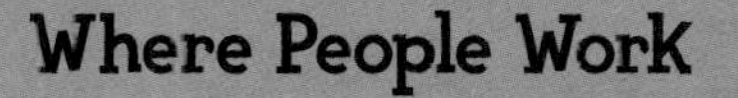

What Happens at an Airport?

By Amy Hutchings

Reading Consultant: Susan Nations, M.Ed.,
author/literacy coach/consultant in literacy development

For a complete list of Where People Work titles,
please visit our web site at **www.garethstevens.com**.
For a free catalog describing Gareth Stevens Publishing's list of high-quality books,
call 1-800-542-2595 (USA) or 1-800-387-3178 (Canada). Our fax: 877-542-2596

Library of Congress Cataloging-in-Publication Data

Hutchings, Amy.
What happens at an airport? / by Amy Hutchings.
p. cm. — (Where people work)
Includes bibliographical references and index.
ISBN-10: 1-4339-0072-6 ISBN-13: 978-1-4339-0072-3 (lib. bdg.)
ISBN-10: 1-4339-0136-6 ISBN-13: 978-1-4339-0136-2 (softcover)
1. Airports—Juvenile literature. 2. Airports—Employees—Juvenile literature.
3. Aeronautics—Vocational guidance—Juvenile literature. I. Title.
TL725.15.H88 2009
387.7'36–dc22 2008023232

This edition first published in 2009 by
Weekly Reader® Books
An Imprint of Gareth Stevens Publishing
1 Reader's Digest Road
Pleasantville, NY 10570-7000 USA

Executive Managing Editor: Lisa M. Herrington
Creative Director: Lisa Donovan
Designers: Alexandria Davis, Jennifer Ryder-Talbot
Photographer: Richard Hutchings
Publisher: Keith Garton

The publisher thanks Stephen Ferguson at the Westchester Airport in White Plains, New York, and JetBlue Airways for their participation in the development of this book.

Printed in the United States of America

1 2 3 4 5 6 7 8 9 10 09 08

Hi, Kids!

I'm Buddy, your Weekly Reader® pal. Have you ever been to an airport? I'm here to show and tell what happens at an airport. So, come on. Turn the page and get ready for takeoff!

Boldface words appear in the glossary.

Airports are busy places. Today Carlos will fly in an airplane. He and his mom are going to visit his aunt.

They check in to get their boarding **tickets**. A worker takes their suitcases to put on the plane.

tickets

Next, they find their **gate**.
A worker takes their tickets.
She shows them where to
get on the plane.

gate

A worker gets the plane ready. The man uses a long hose to put **fuel** into the plane.

fuel

A worker loads suitcases onto the plane. The bags travel along a moving belt.

A **flight attendant** greets Carlos and his mom. He will help them find their seats.

flight attendant

Carlos and his mom pass the **cockpit**. The cockpit is the area where the **pilot** sits.

pilot
cockpit

It is time for takeoff!
A worker helps the big
plane onto the **runway**.

runway
Blue Kid in Town

The airplane takes off from the runway. Many people make an airport work!

Glossary

cockpit: the area at the front of the plane where the pilot sits

flight attendant: a person who helps passengers and serves food and drinks on a plane

fuel: gasoline that is used to power the plane

gate: the entrance to get on the plane and the area where the plane parks

pilot: a person who flies a plane

runway: a strip of land that planes use for taking off and landing

tickets: papers that show a fee has been paid

For More Information

Books

DK Big Book of Airplanes. Anne Millard (DK Publishing, 2001)

First Plane Trip. Fred Bear and Friends (series). Melanie Joyce (Gareth Stevens Publishing, 2008)

Web Sites

AvKids.com

www.avkids.com/hangar/smartparts

Explore the parts of a plane with an exciting activity.

FAA Kids' Corner

www.faa.gov/education_research/education/student_resources/kids_corner

Check out fun activities about airplanes.

Publisher's note to educators and parents: Our editors have carefully reviewed these web sites to ensure that they are suitable for children. Many web sites change frequently, however, and we cannot guarantee that a site's future contents will continue to meet our high standards of quality and educational value. Be advised that children should be closely supervised whenever they access the Internet.

Index

About the Author

Amy Hutchings was part of the original production staff of *Sesame Street* for the first ten years of the show's history. She then went on to work with her husband, Richard, producing thousands of photographs for children's publishers. She has written several books, including *Firehouse Dog* and *Picking Apples and Pumpkins*. She lives in Rhinebeck, New York, along with many deer, squirrels, and wild turkeys.